cross stitch
Flower Models

Lesley Teare

Project Gallery

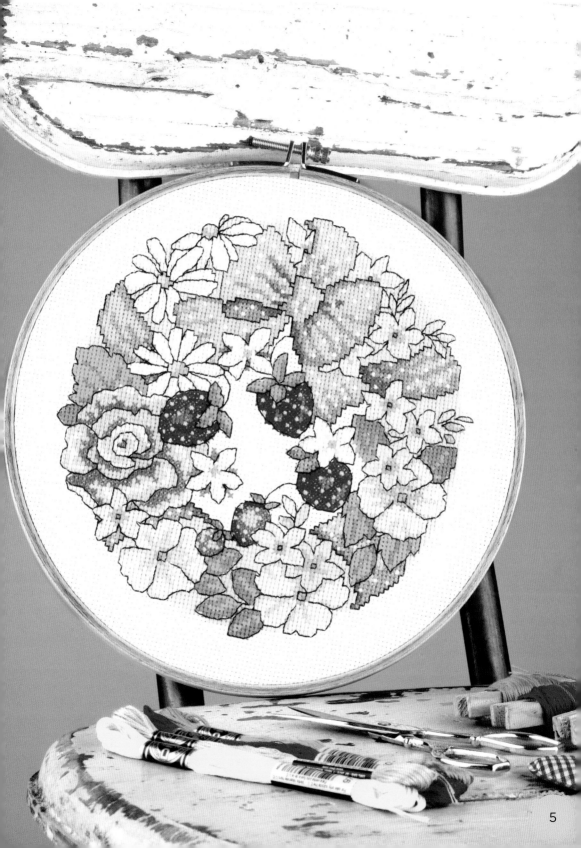

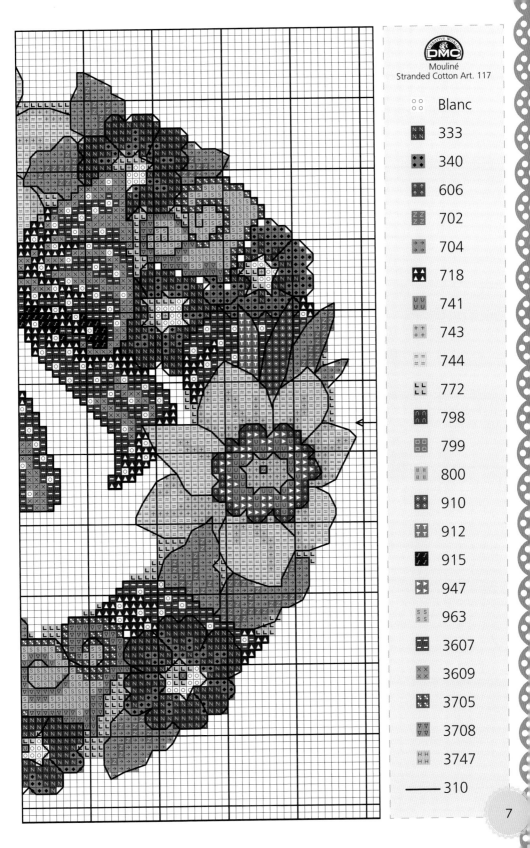

DMC
Mouliné
Stranded Cotton Art. 117

::	Blanc
N N	333
◆◆	340
↑↑	606
Z Z	702
→→	704
▲▲	718
U U	741
++	743
==	744
L L	772
∩∩	798
□□	799
‖ ‖	800
◉◉	910
T T	912
∕∕	915
✳✳	947
S S	963
⊞⊞	3607
××	3609
∴∴	3705
▽▽	3708
H H	3747
——	310

DMC
Mouliné
Stranded Cotton Art. 117

○ ○	Blanc
✱ ✱	321
↑ ↑	606
Z Z	702
→ →	704
U U	741
+ +	743
= =	744
L L	772
∩ ∩	798
□ □	799
II II	800
◉ ◉	910
◄►	947
S S	963
✖ ✖	3705
▽ ▽	3708
H H	3747
——	310

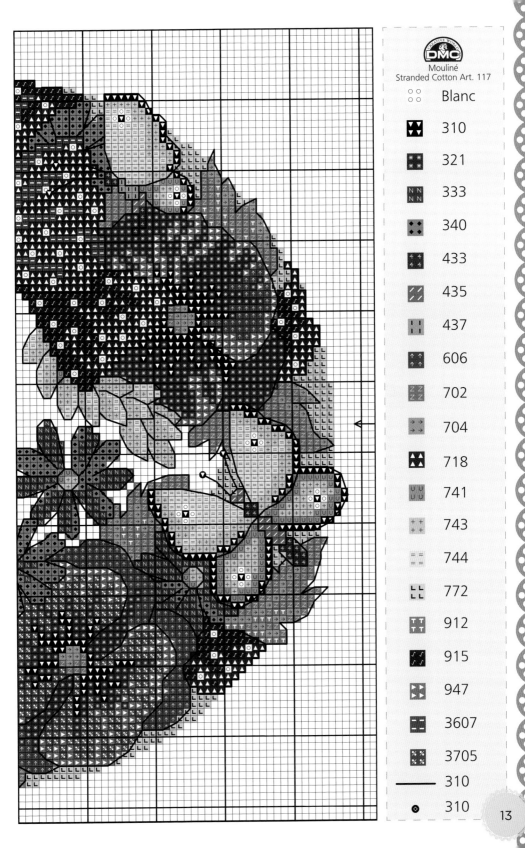

DMC
Mouliné
Stranded Cotton Art. 117

○○ ○○	Blanc
	310
	321
N N N N	333
	340
4 4 4 4	433
	435
I I I I	437
↑ ↑	606
Z Z Z Z	702
→ → → →	704
	718
U U U U	741
+ + + +	743
= = = =	744
L L L L	772
T T T T	912
	915
	947
	3607
╳ ╳ ╳ ╳	3705
——	310
◆	310

13

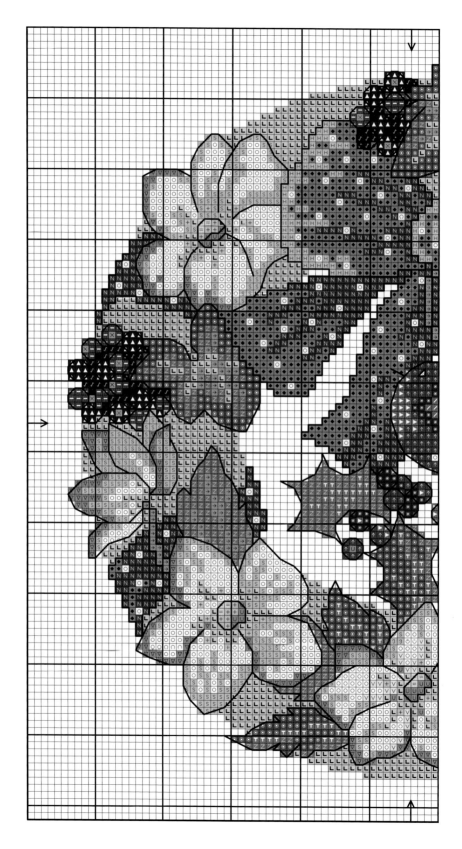

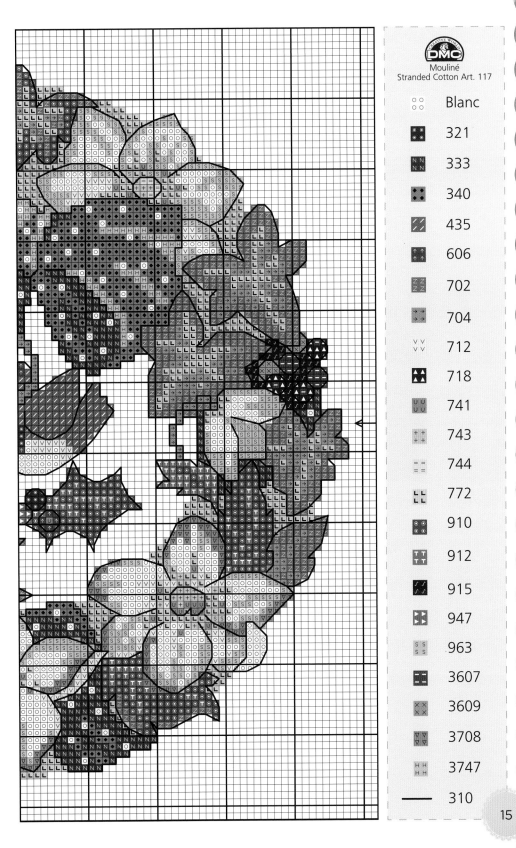

DMC
Mouliné
Stranded Cotton Art. 117

○ ○	Blanc
✱ ✱	321
N N	333
◆ ◆	340
╱╱	435
↑ ↑	606
Z Z	702
→ →	704
v v	712
▲ ▲	718
U U	741
+ +	743
= =	744
L L	772
⊙ ⊙	910
T T	912
╱	915
◆ ◆	947
s s	963
▪ ▪	3607
× ×	3609
▽ ▽	3708
H H	3747
——	310

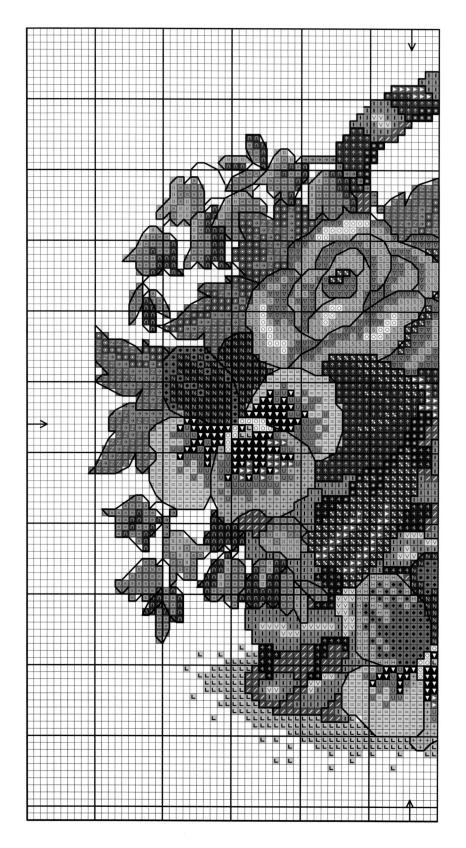

DMC
Mouliné
Stranded Cotton Art. 117

° °	Blanc
▲▼	310
✳ ✳	321
N N	333
◆ ◆	340
4 4	433
∕ ∕	435
I I	437
↑ ↑	606
Z Z	702
→ →	704
v v	712
U U	741
+ +	743
= =	744
L L	772
∩ ∩	798
□ □	799
II II	800
● ●	910
✖	947
s s	963
✖ ✖	3705
▽ ▽	3708
H H	3747
——	310

19

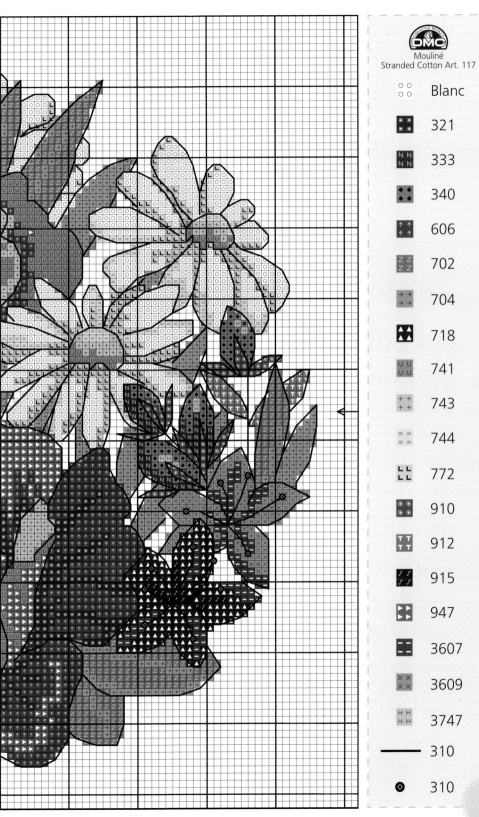

Mouliné
Stranded Cotton Art. 117

Symbol	Color
○ ○	Blanc
✷ ✷	321
N N	333
◆ ◆	340
↑ ↑	606
Z Z	702
→ →	704
▲▲	718
U U	741
+ +	743
= =	744
L L	772
⊙ ⊙	910
T T	912
◢ ◢	915
▶▶	947
▬ ▬	3607
✕ ✕	3609
H H	3747
——	310
◈	310

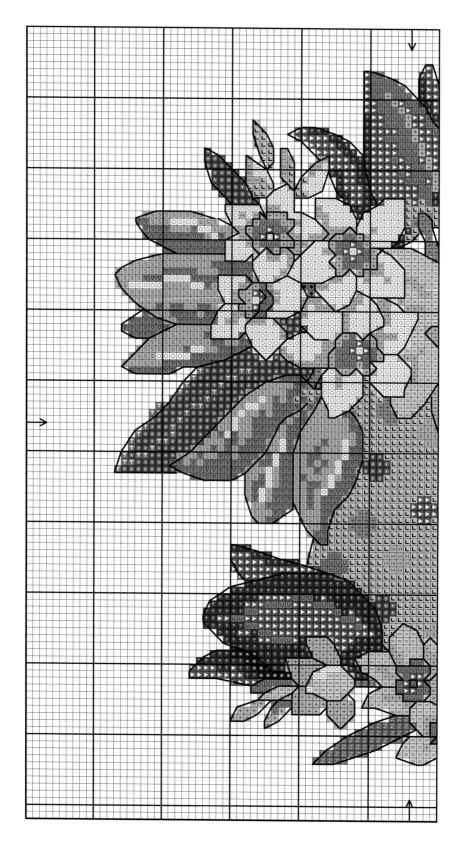

DMC
Mouliné
Stranded Cotton Art. 117

° ° / ° °	Blanc
* * / * *	321
⬥⬥ / ⬥⬥	340
↑ ↑ / ↑ ↑	606
Z Z / Z Z	702
→ → / → →	704
U U / U U	741
+ + / + +	743
= = / = =	744
L L / L L	772
‖ ‖ / ‖ ‖	800
◉ ◉ / ◉ ◉	910
T T / T T	912
◣◤ / ◣◤	947
S S / S S	963
▽ ▽ / ▽ ▽	3708
H H / H H	3747
——	310

DMC
Mouliné
Stranded Cotton Art. 117

Symbol	DMC
∘ ∘	Blanc
♥ ♥	310
∗ ∗	321
N N	333
∙ ∙	340
4 4	433
∕ ∕	435
Z Z	702
→ →	704
♠ ♠	718
U U	741
+ +	743
= =	744
L L	772
⊙ ⊙	910
T T	912
∕ ∕	915
⊞ ⊞	947
S S	963
▮ ▮	3607
× ×	3609
※ ※	3705
▽ ▽	3708
H H	3747
—	310
◈	310

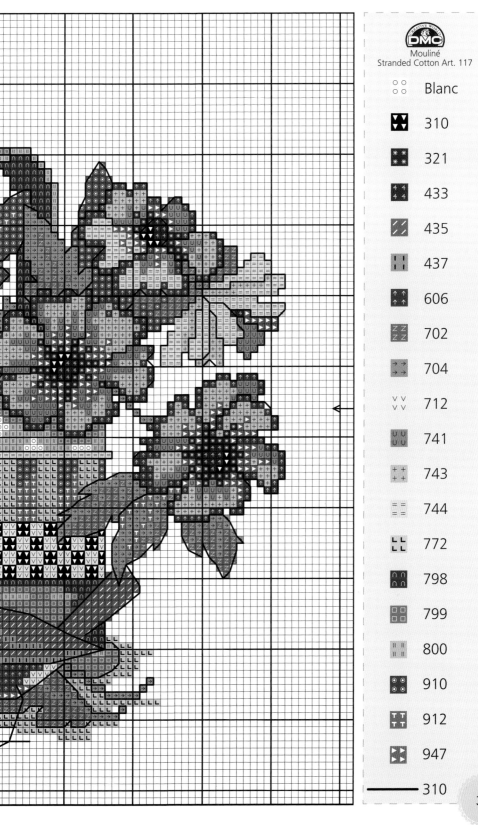

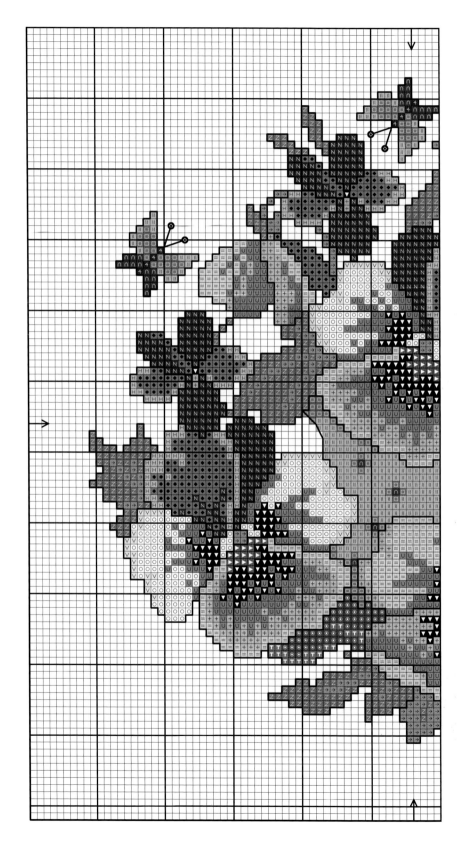

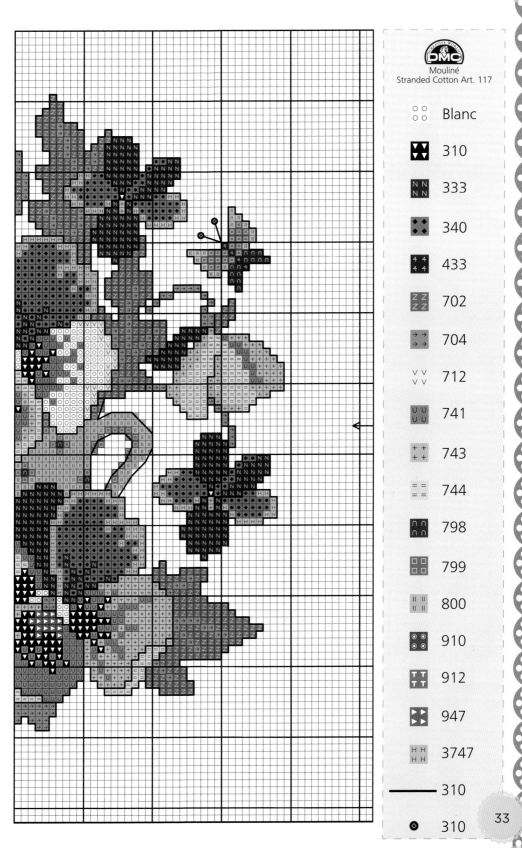

DMC
Mouliné
Stranded Cotton Art. 117

Symbol	Code
° ° / ° °	Blanc
▼▼ / ▼▼	310
N N / N N	333
◆ ◆ / ◆ ◆	340
4 4 / 4 4	433
Z Z / Z Z	702
→ → / → →	704
V V / V V	712
U U / U U	741
+ + / + +	743
= = / = =	744
∩ ∩ / ∩ ∩	798
□ □ / □ □	799
‖ ‖ / ‖ ‖	800
⊚ ⊚ / ⊚ ⊚	910
T T / T T	912
◄► / ◄►	947
H H / H H	3747
——	310
◉	310

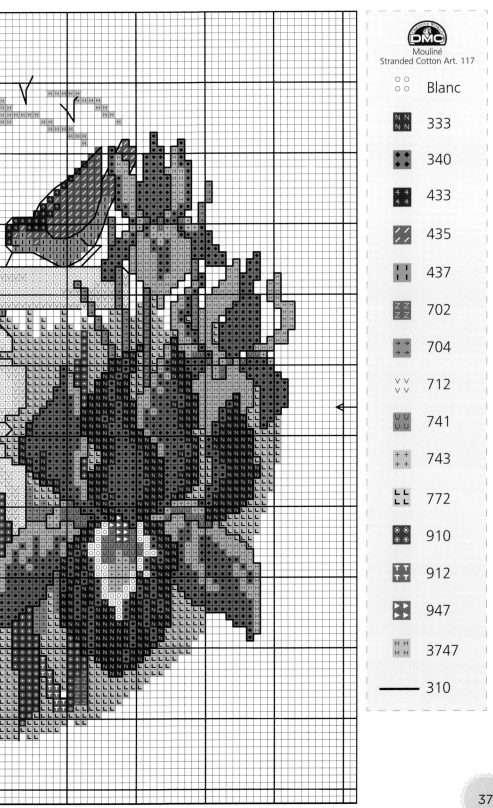

DMC
Mouliné
Stranded Cotton Art. 117

○ ○ ○ ○	Blanc
N N N N	333
✦ ✦ ✦ ✦	340
4 4 4 4	433
╱ ╱ ╱ ╱	435
I I I I	437
Z Z Z Z	702
→ → → →	704
V V V V	712
U U U U	741
+ + + +	743
L L L L	772
◉ ◉ ◉ ◉	910
T T T T	912
✖ ✖ ✖ ✖	947
H H H H	3747
——	310

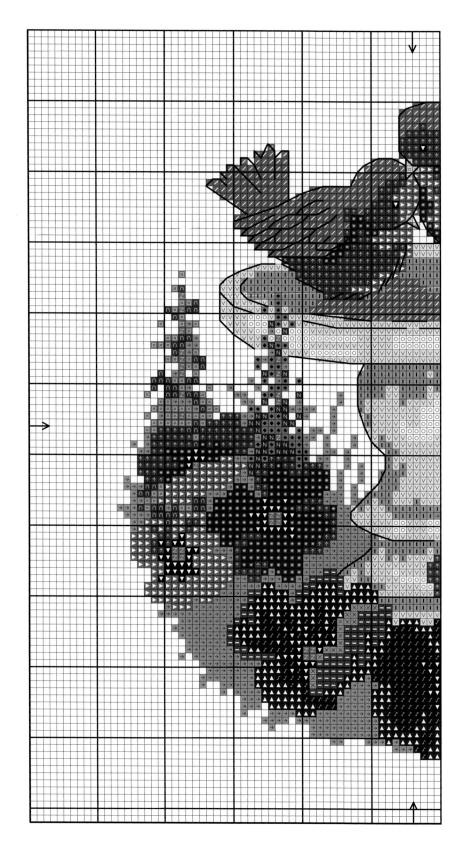

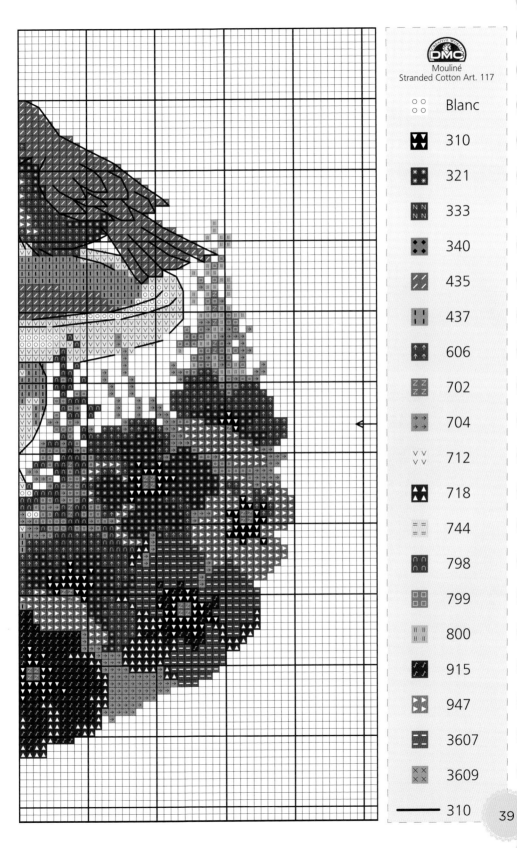

DMC
Mouliné
Stranded Cotton Art. 117

Symbol	Color
° °	Blanc
310	310
✱ ✱	321
N N	333
◆ ◆	340
⁄ ⁄	435
I I	437
↑ ↑	606
Z Z	702
→ →	704
V V	712
718	718
═ ═	744
∩ ∩	798
□ □	799
‖ ‖	800
⁄ ⁄	915
947	947
▬ ▬	3607
X X	3609
——	310

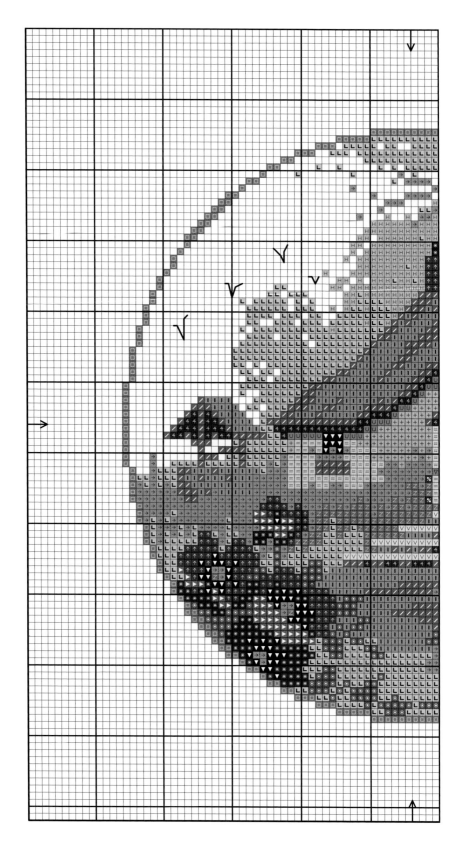

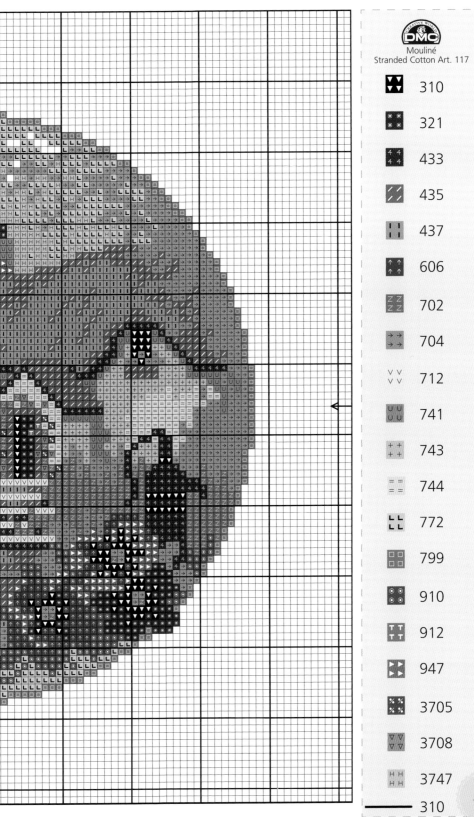

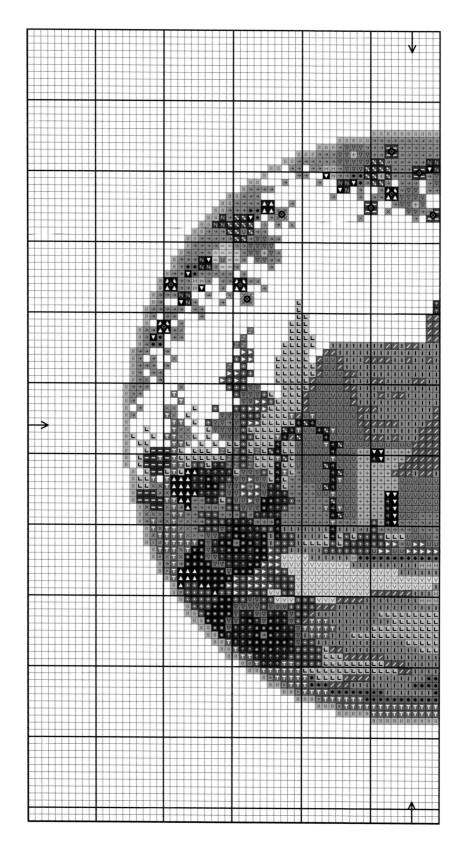

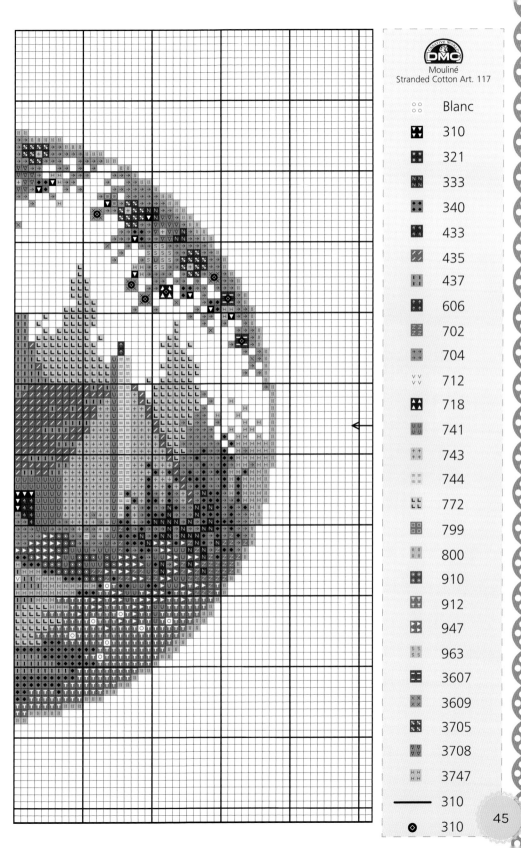

DMC

Mouliné
Stranded Cotton Art. 117

Symbol	Color
○ ○	Blanc
	310
	321
N N / N N	333
	340
4 / 4 4	433
/ /	435
	437
↑ ↑	606
Z / Z Z	702
→ / →	704
V V / V V	712
	718
U U / U U	741
+ + / + +	743
= = / = =	744
L L / L L	772
□ □ / □ □	799
‖ ‖ / ‖ ‖	800
	910
T T / T T	912
	947
S S / S S	963
	3607
X X / X X	3609
	3705
▼ ▼ / ▼ ▼	3708
H H / H H	3747
——	310
◉	310

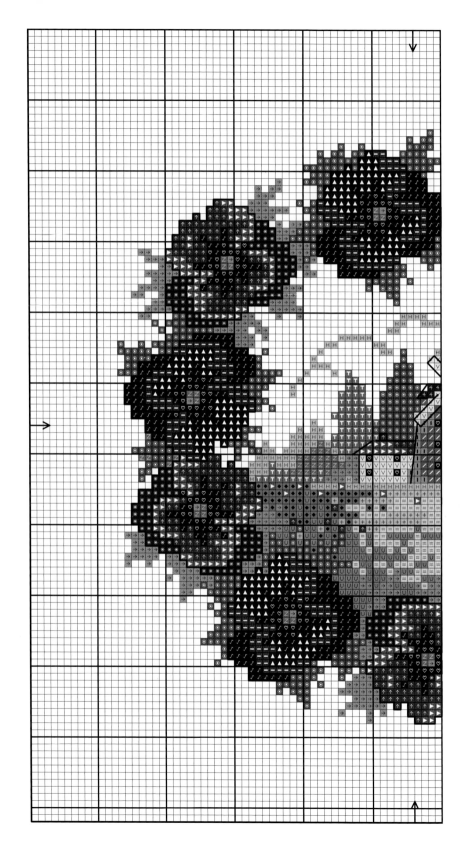

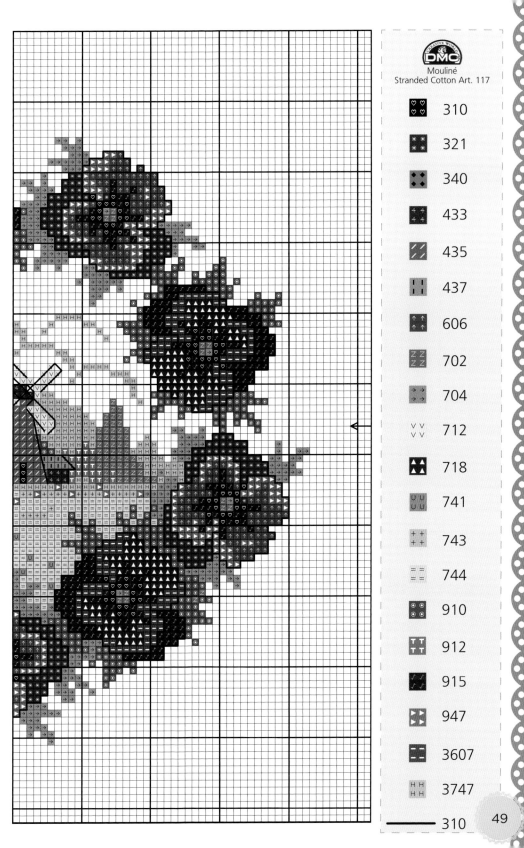

DMC
Mouliné
Stranded Cotton Art. 117

Symbol	Code
♥♥ / ♥♥	310
✳✳ / ✳✳	321
◆◆ / ◆◆	340
4 4 / 4 4	433
∕∕ / ∕∕	435
I I / I I	437
↑↑ / ↑↑	606
Z Z / Z Z	702
→ → / → →	704
V V / V V	712
▲▲ / ▲▲	718
U U / U U	741
+ + / + +	743
= = / = =	744
◉◉ / ◉◉	910
T T / T T	912
∕∕ / ∕∕	915
▶▶ / ▶▶	947
▬▬ / ▬▬	3607
H H / H H	3747

───── 310

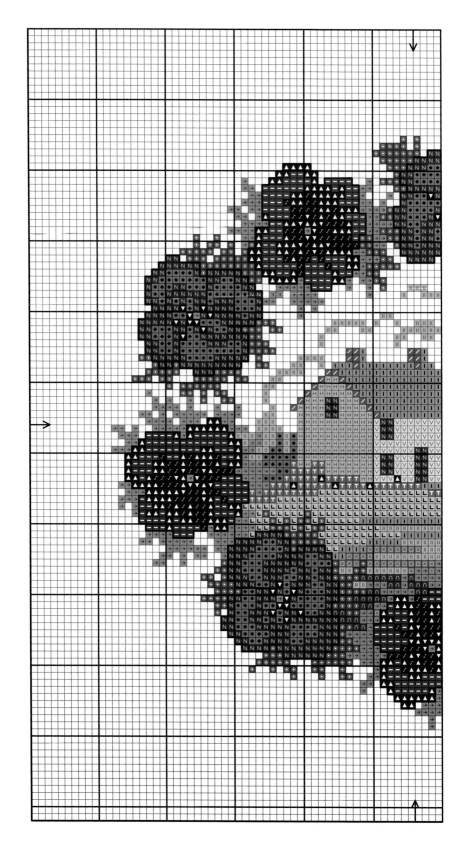

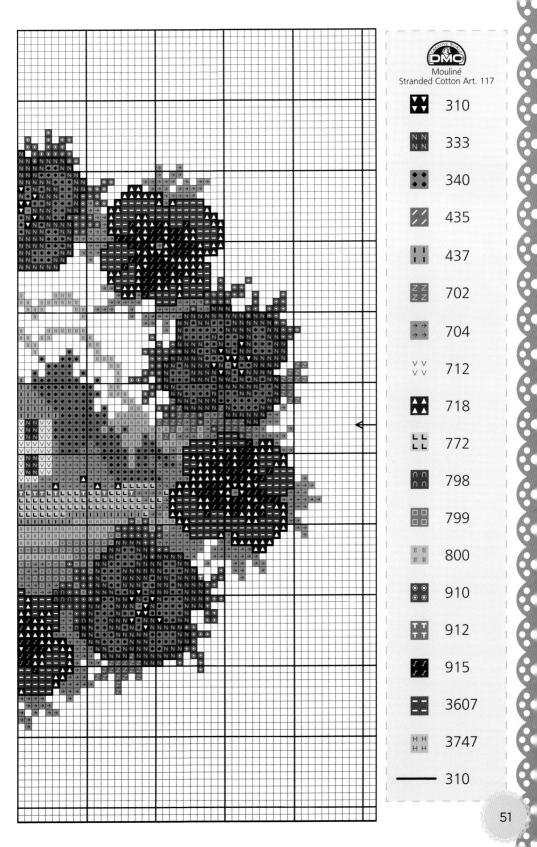

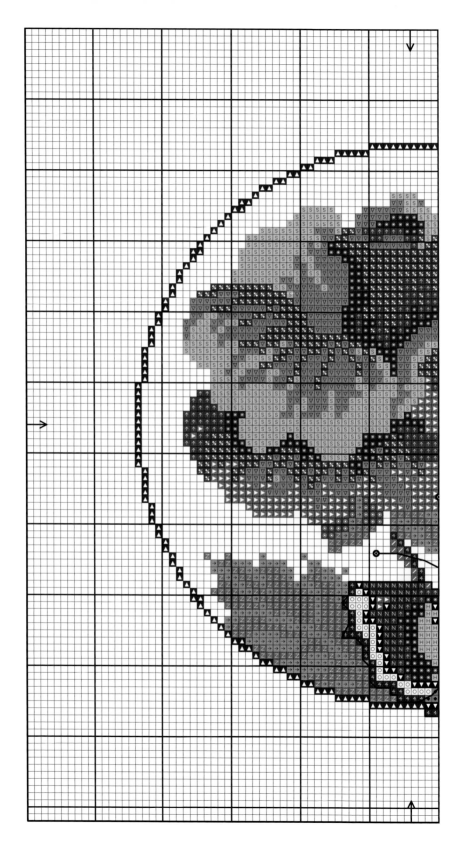

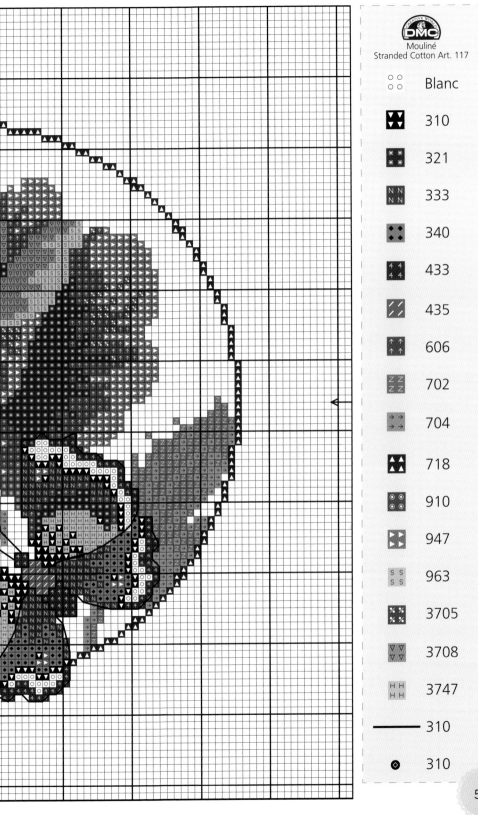

DMC
Mouliné
Stranded Cotton Art. 117

Symbol	Color
○○ ○○	Blanc
▲▲ ▲▲	310
✳✳ ✳✳	321
N N N N	333
◆◆ ◆◆	340
4 4 4 4	433
╱╱ ╱╱	435
↑↑ ↑↑	606
Z Z Z Z	702
→→ →→	704
▲▲ ▲▲	718
◎◎ ◎◎	910
✦✦ ✦✦	947
S S S S	963
✺✺ ✺✺	3705
▽▽ ▽▽	3708
H H H H	3747
——	310
◈	310

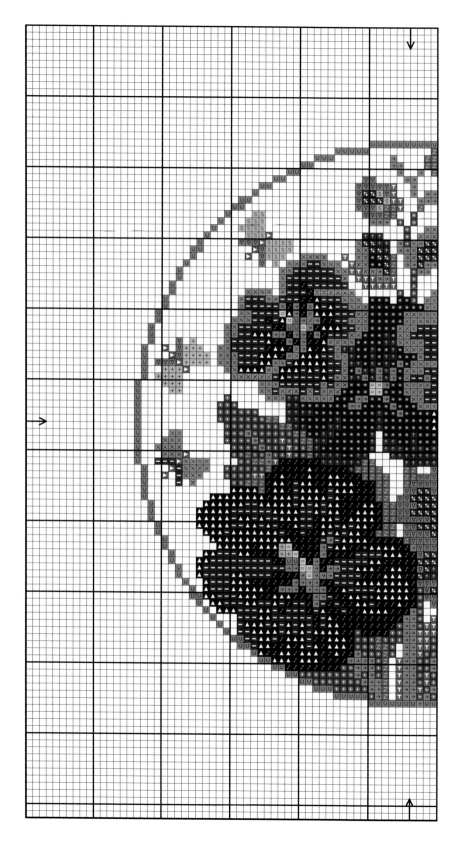

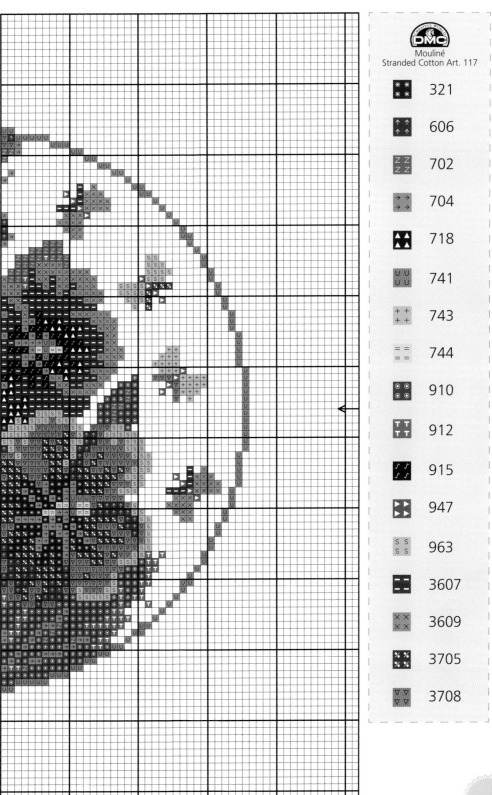

DMC
Mouliné
Stranded Cotton Art. 117

✳✳ ✳✳	321
↑↑ ↑↑	606
ZZ ZZ	702
→→ →→	704
▲▲	718
UU UU	741
++ ++	743
== ==	744
◉◉ ◉◉	910
TT TT	912
⁄⁄	915
►►	947
SS SS	963
▬▬	3607
×× ××	3609
٪٪ ٪٪	3705
▽▽ ▽▽	3708

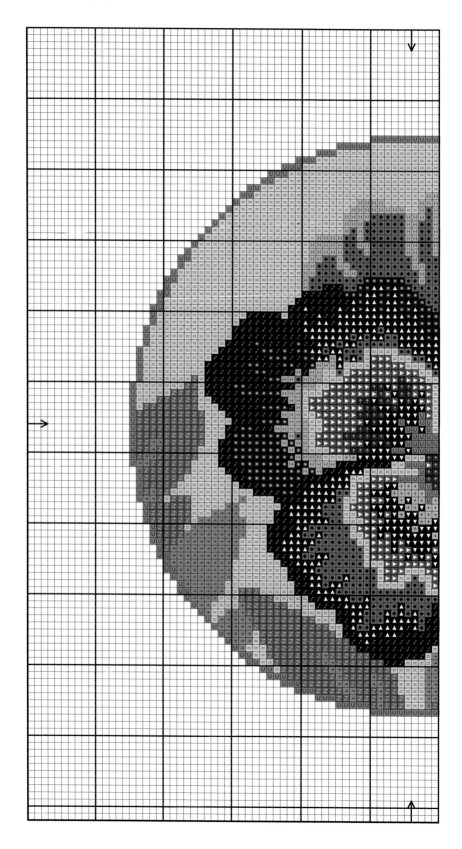

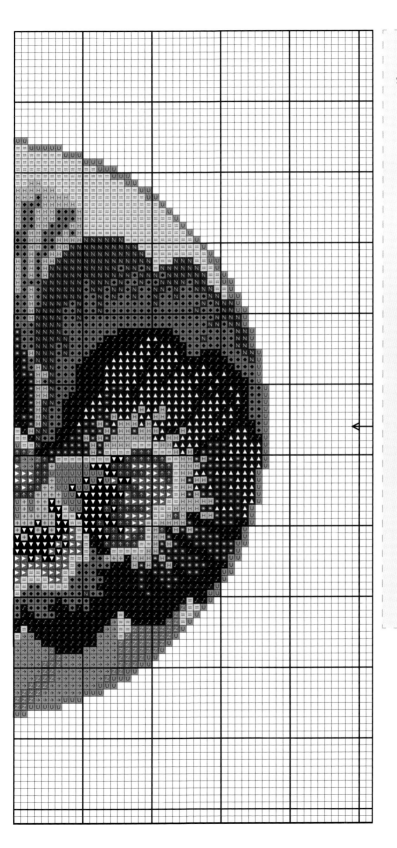

DMC
Mouliné
Stranded Cotton Art. 117

	310
	321
N N / N N	333
	340
↑ ↑ / ↑ ↑	606
Z Z / Z Z	702
→ → / → →	704
	718
U U / U U	741
+ + / + +	743
= = / = =	744
	915
	947
H H / H H	3747

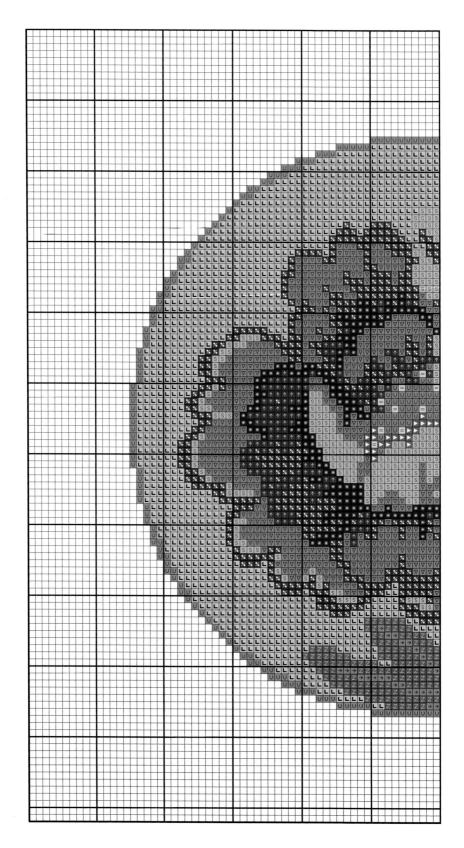

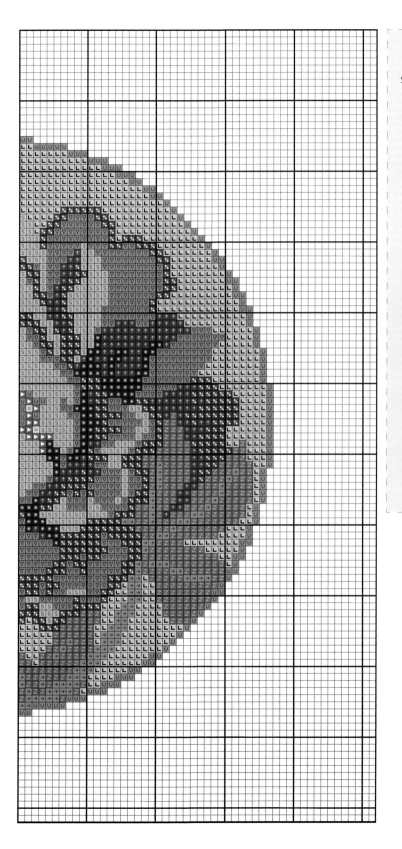

Mouliné
Stranded Cotton Art. 117

Symbol	Color
✱ ✱	321
↑ ↑	606
Z Z	702
→ →	704
U U	741
= =	744
L L	772
◄►	947
S S	963
✄ ✄	3705
▽ ▽	3708